All Scripture references taken from the KJV of the Holy Bible unless otherwise indicated.

Tormenting Spirits by Dr. Marlene Miles

Freshwater Press, USA

ISBN: 978-1-960150-58-5

Paperback Version

Copyright 2023 by Dr. Marlene Miles

All rights reserved. No part of this book may be reproduced, distributed or transmitted by any means or in any means including photocopying, recording or other electronic or mechanical methods without prior written permission of the publisher except in the case of brief publications or critical reviews.

Table of Contents

Fear Has Torment 4
When Man Loses Authority 10
Deaf & Dumb *Spirits* 17
Turned Over to the Tormentors 27
The Stone Rolled Back 30
Unforgiveness Has Torment 35
Prison 38
Soul Ties 42
The Thing I Greatly Feared 49
Fragmented Soul 55
Closure 58
Love Has No Torment 71
Warfare Prayers 74
Dear Reader 93
Christian books by this author 94

Tormenting Spirits

Fear Has Torment

Fear has torment. There's No Fear in love but perfect love casts out fear, because fear hath torment. He that feareth is not made perfect in love, (John 4:18).

Now the spirit of the Lord departed from Saul, and an evil spirit terrorized him. Saul's servants said to him, Behold now an evil spirit from God is terrorizing you. Let … your servants…..seek a man who is a skillful player on the harp, and … when the evil spirit …is on you. that he shall play the harp …and you will be well.

(1 Samuel 16:14-16, excerpted)

Here, the evil spirit is not from God; it is *allowed* by God.

I linger on verse 14 now: The *Spirit of the Lord departed from Saul.* I wonder which is worse, when the Spirit of the Lord departs from a person, or if a person never had the Spirit of the Lord in the first place. Then I ask, *Why would the Spirit of the Lord leave a man, or leave any person?*

Disobedience, sin, unrepentant person, repetitive sin, *(Deuteronomy 28, Choose ye this day.)* are reasons why the Spirit of the Lord would leave a person. The Spirit of the Lord will leave when a man's own choices do not please God. That man wants to do it his way, live life his way, and he repeatedly chooses to sin. God will turn His back on the man who is frolicking in his own free will. God has given us free will, so you and I, and that man can do what he wants to do, the way he wants to do it, go where he wants to, and live his life the way he chooses without regard to God. Some do this knowingly, others are deceived, thinking that if you get saved, you're good until death and anything goes in the meantime. That is not true.

God has already made it clear what He will do and what He won't do, where He will go and where God will not go. God in His Word has made it clear what He'll bless and what He will not bless. And because God doesn't look on sin, neither He nor His Spirit will go where there's repetitive sin.

In the course of repetitive sin, a man's guardian Angel from the Lord, departs from a human, then a *guardian demon* is substituted. That seems to be what happened to Saul. The Spirit of the Lord departed from Saul, and he became quite demonized.

We know from the New Testament that when a house is found empty, that is, the Holy Spirit is not there, then here come the squatters. Here come the evil *spirits* of darkness to live in that *house*, in that empty house, that dry place. And I'm saying that something should be in the place where the Spirit of the Lord should reside in you. If nothing is there, it is as though the door is left open, it is empty, that is the same as being swept clean. Anything could come in; the devil sends in unclean and evil spirits, immediately.

I'm also saying that if you have received deliverance from ungodly spirits, when you get rid of all evil *spirits*, you must replace the loss--, even though they were evil spirits, you must replace them with something. Ideally, that space in man is made for the Holy Spirit of God. However, if nothing else is there, then the *spirit* that the man was just delivered from will try to come back. It will remember your location, unfortunately. And it will try to come back. The Bible says that *spirit* will bring seven more evil spirits like it or worse than it. So now the problem is far worse.

After cleansing and deliverance from evil *spirits*, we must always ask for the infilling and/or a re-filling of the Holy Spirit. A man should then submit to the Holy Spirit and live upright before the Lord to keep this or worse from happening again.

Man was made to commune intimately with God, he was made to worship God. There is a place *in* man for the Spirit of God. There is a place in man for worship, for intimacy and relationship with God. But if you don't have or lose the Spirit of God, there will be a void inside of you. If the Spirit of God departs from you or you are person who's never accepted Jesus Christ as your Lord and Savior and received the infilling of the Holy Spirit, then there is an empty place in you. That empty space will be as a vacuum that just sucks the **world** right into it because we are in the world, so that's the default.

God has given man dominion over the Earth. We were formed from Earth, so we must conduct ourselves properly and possess our vessels (our bodies) in sanctification and honor.

If we do not, by default, evil will be sucked right into that place where God should be. When God comes down to commune with a man, as He did with

Adam, in the cool of the day, God will not have to again ask, ***"Adam, where are you?"***

If that place where **God** should be, the place that God *made* for man to allow His Spirit to reside is inhabited with unclean squatting *spirits*, then that man is considered polluted. Evil will be there instead. God will not stay in that squalor. That's the first "earth" we should take authority over, our own bodies.

When Man Loses Authority

Constantly, night and day he was screaming among the tombs in the mountains, gashing himself with stones, (Mark 5:5)

This verse is about Legion in the Gadarenes, who was inhabited by so many evil *spirits* that he was hurting himself; he was possessed. The Spirit of the Lord protects, keeps, helps, guides, leads a man into truth and righteousness.

Evil spirits are sent to steal, kill and destroy a man. They may entice by making it seem exciting at first, but the demons' goal is to steal, kill, and destroy.

Let's go back to Saul. David ran from Saul for more than a decade because Saul wanted to kill David. Saul was jealous of David, envious of David, worried about David, obsessed with David for more than a dozen years. There is no way Saul would have been hunting David while the Spirit of God was within Saul.

That was a tormenting spirit, or tormenting spirits. Those spirits tormented Saul and in return, Saul tormented David˜˜, for years. **Tormented people torment people.**

Saul had been anointed of God and the Spirit of the Lord had been placed on Saul when he was selected to be king. It was more likely that Saul had *lost* the Spirit of God and was jealous and despised the Spirit in David.

For this reason, you should know that when people hate you for no reason, it is most likely that they are demonized, and you being God's own.--, they hate the Spirit within you. Jesus said, **Marvel not, they hated Me first,** (John 15:18, *emphasis added, mine*).

In general there are sins and attitudes that will drive the Spirit of God away from man. Yeah, the big 10, --the Ten Commandments. We've all sinned and fallen short of the Glory of God, but to repeatedly break any one of these Commandments grieves the Holy Spirit. Grieve not the Holy Spirit – because He will leave you, over time.

The 10 Commandments are from the Book of Exodus, and there are also commandments in the New Testament. This book will spend some time on some of the sins of the New Testament. They are unforgiveness, bitterness, resentment and strife. Additionally, in the longest sentence (maybe ever), they are: blaspheming God and the Holy Spirit, boasting, brutality, taking a brother in the Faith to court, carousing, clamoring, complaining, conceit, coveting, cowardice, deceit, defrauding your brother, denying Christ, desiring the praise of men, disobedience, divisions, drinking, parties, revelries, drunkenness, having Holy Communion undeservedly, egotism, enmities, envy, evil thoughts, lying, lying on someone, provoking your own child to wrath, fear, filthiness, fleshiness, foolishness, fornication, greed, lust, being a hater, perversion, sexual perversions, hypocrisy, idolatry, impurity, jealousy, jesting, judging, knowing to do good but not doing it, laying up treasures on Earth, living for pleasure, lusting, malice, murder, murmuring, pride, prostitution, quarrels, reveling, reviling dignities, sensuality, slander, sorcery, stealing, swearing, swindling, treachery, unbelief, ungodliness, ungratefulness, unholiness, unrighteousness, wickedness, wrath. These things will drive the Spirit of God away from a man, away from a woman, away from a person. Can you also see that the actions associated with these sins include torment? The desire might be to torment the object of your hatred or jealousy, or issue, but the perpetrator of the sin invites Torment by doing the sin. He may want the Torment to be transferred to his believed enemy, and it might be, but the sinner gets it too.

Evil is equal opportunity. Evil spirits don't care who you are; you have no control over them except by Jesus Christ.

Of course, all those sins are bad, but mostly in this book we will deal with Unforgiveness.

People don't forgive for a number of reasons. One of the reasons is pride. You will be hard pressed to get a person full of pride to forgive.

If they're full of hate, they won't forgive.

If they're jealous, they can't forgive. If they are in fear--, the same. Remember, **fear has torment**. Fear brings torment to a sinner, if they won't forgive.

If they are hurt, they won't forgive.

When a person wants to enact their own vengeance, for any reason, maybe none of the above reasons, they are just mean spirited, instead of offering mercy or grace, they won't forgive.

Bitterness, unforgiveness and strife, I think, are the biggest three, the biggest blockers to people getting healing or getting their deliverance and becoming free from Torment.

Back to King Saul. The Spirit of the Lord departed from him because of disobedience. He was in a battle where he had been instructed by God to destroy everything, but he brought the captured king from the battle back to the camp. He brought back the fatted cattle and sheep. Worse, Saul was out in the field during the battle doing sacrifices, ***without*** Samuel, without the Prophet, the priest of God. Saul was not supposed to be doing any of that. This was stone cold disobedience.

Saul hated David; he was jealous of David, he had murder in his heart toward

David, and he also sought a witch at Endor. God hates witchcraft.

Deaf & Dumb *Spirits*

Saul started out good, head and shoulders above the rest. But he was disobedient, and greedy, and tried to cover up his greed with excuses of all kinds. You cannot trick God. Even though Saul started out well, he changed up on God, but God didn't miss that. At first Saul was obedient, but then he became disobedient, later he used his position to do as he wanted to do and did not follow the directives of God.

As stated, from the aforementioned battle, Saul had not killed Agag, the king of the Amalekites. And he (Saul) had saved sheep and cattle for sacrifice; but that's not what God told him to do. And that is where the verse, *To obey is better than to sacrifice came from.*

So, God pulled His Spirit from Saul, which means Saul also lost God's anointing. We can learn from what happened with Saul that God judges us by our inward, by the inward man, not by what we *look* like. Remember, Saul was good looking. God judges the heart, and God wants us to have confidence in Him, not in just *self*, and not to be boastful and prideful. It is God's will that we should be following, not our own selfish will.

God commands that we follow His commandments, all of them, and not just cherry pick the ones we like. People who cherry pick the Commandments of God, are probably picking from other religions too and blending them all together. That is idolatry. This is not pure worship of and service to God. He is not pleased with that.

There are some people who are affected with a *deaf and dumb spirit,* and they just don't listen to instructions. The

Proverbs beg over and over again, **Hear wisdom, get understanding,** get some common sense. My mom said that to us all the time, *Get common sense*, and we didn't know what she was talking about, but now that we are older, now we do.

There are some people who are suffering under *deaf and dumb spirits*. From the New Testament we may think it's where the person can't talk, they can't speak as in the case of that little boy that was being thrown into the fire by evil *spirits*.

Those are gross manifestations of that deaf and dumb *spirit*, but there are less severe cases of it. I'm talking about a mild case where a person just doesn't listen to instructions. That's a *spirit*. Bind it up and cast it out, in Jesus' Name.

It could be that this *deaf and dumb spirit* is responsible for disobedience and for unfaithfulness to God. People under this oppression are slow to learn life's lessons. They're slow to see life's patterns.

They're slow to see spiritual problems and natural patterns in life. They can **watch** somebody, in person, going through a thing, in real time, and never learn a thing from it.

Oh, it can happen.

It happened to me when I was really young, like in my early 20's. I remember somebody showed and told me something right to my face. They hid nothing about what they were saying. They gave me the honest truth, but it took me a year or two years later to go, *Oh, that's what they were saying to me.*

Hey, it's a *spirit.* We have to bind that up, even in ourselves. Sometimes **we** need deliverance.

- Every *spirit of deaf and dumb* following me for years, pack your crap and get out of my life, in the Name of Jesus.

The *deaf and dumb spirit* is a *tormenting spirit,* a demonic *spirit.* They are unclean *spirits,* and they are Tormentors. And they will torment a man, a woman, a person, and cause afflictions.

The word, *torment* here means *to torture, to twist, strain, or vex.*

We want to be pleasing to God. We don't want our life to be in vain or wasted. We don't want to be a useless vessel or a vessel of dishonor. We need to possess our vessel in sanctification and honor. We do that by hearing and obeying God.

It doesn't take God as long as it takes most of us to realize that somebody has **rejected** us. Now, I'm not saying that we're supposed to harbor *spirits of rejection.* I'm just saying we need to know when to and how to move on, in Jesus Name. Keep it moving.

When we reject God as Saul did--, if we reject God, He will pull His Spirit away from us. God is longsuffering and patient, but at the same time He keeps it moving. God moves in perfect balance, always.

Unfortunately, when God pulls His Spirit, though, that is what gives opportunity for the evil squatters to come into your life, into your body, into your house, into your whole situation. So if we reject God, God will reject us. If God is not in our lives, it's as though we are unguarded, unprotected and anything goes, as far as the devil is concerned.

God deals with us all according to our own hearts. So a stubborn, hard-headed, egotistical, self-willed person who only wants to do it his way may be told, *Oh, you want to do it your way?* Well go ahead, see how that works out for you. God is kind of like that. If we show signs of a seared conscience, He may turn us over to a reprobate mind if we insist on sinning and being disobedient to His Word. He is loving, kind, patient, merciful and gracious, but if a person **keeps** sinning, if we keep doing wrong, He may say, **Have it your way**.

Before He does that, He tries to bring us under conviction and turn us to the right way, by the Holy Spirit, leading us to repentance.

But--, the devil tries to condemn man, and then if he can get those *tormenting spirits*, into your life, he will keep tormenting you until you're dead.

Being in a physical prison in the natural might be better than getting turned over to the devil, because sometimes people get *out* of jail in the natural. However, being in jail or prison in the natural is often a **sign** that a person is already captive in the spiritual realm. Life flows from the Spiritual realm into the natural realm.

Once the devil gets a hold of a human, he plans to keep him forever--, until they are dead. A human is nothing to the devil, nothing. A man, a woman, a person means nothing to the devil.

Torment is defined as *twisting, straining, extreme pain, anguish*, the utmost degree of misery, body misery, or mental anguish. Torment is anything that gives you pain, vexation, or misery.

In the New Testament, the sick people who were bought to Jesus were described has having different kinds of diseases and *torments*, the Word says in Matthew 4. This proves that if your *spirit* man is not strong enough, if you're not filled with the Holy Spirit of God, then a vexing and a tormenting evil *spirit* will try to come and take up residence in your life.

An ***infirmity*** is a usual consequence, or a big sign that Torment is what's happening to you, whether it's your own fault or by an open door. It could be by an evil or a weak foundation, an ancestral curse, something you inherited, by no fault of yours. But if it's happening to you, and you see it, and you know it, and you are teachable, then we can do something about it. Fire prayers.

Even if **you** have done nothing to cause spiritual attacks to come upon you, the devil will send in Tormentors, strongmen when there are ***spiritual debts*** owed down your family line. That's how they communicate – it's kind of Guido-like, but <u>that is the language.</u> You could have done nothing **AT ALL**, but here comes an unsolicited, unexpected attack.

To better understand this, let's say you come out from your job or shopping, and someone has vandalized your car, keyed it and spray-painted obscenities on it. You have not parked over the line or bumped into their car; you've done **nothing**. It's like that.

Violence is their language.

You have NO IDEA that any spiritual debt was owed down your family line. Your parents and your grandparents on both sides treated you like gold. You had no idea there was *sin*, and most of all unrepented sin, unsettled sin debts on any side of your family. Nobody sent you a colorful envelope with Final Notice stamped on it.

But there is this attack. Barbaric, actually.

Turned Over to the Tormentors

And his Lord was wroth and delivered him to the tormentors, (KJV). So he should pay all that was due unto him. (Matthew 18:34).

...delivered him to the tormentors--, the NIV version says, *jailers*.

And the Lord was angry and delivered him to the tormentors until he should pay all that was due to him. A man was forgiven a great deal of money, but when that man's servants owed him a small amount of money, the newly forgiven man did not forgive the servant. Instead, the well-off and forgiven man threw the servant into jail. Jail is where the tormentors are. The man that was forgiven a lot still wanted to *be* a tormentor, or at least <u>see</u> another tormented.

God may have said something like, ***Really, you gonna do that? I'm gonna deal with you according to your own heart.*** God took the guy that owed a little bit of money out of jail and put the man that was forgiven so much *into* jail.

And his lord was wroth, and delivered him to the tormentors, till he should pay all that was due unto him. Matthew 18:34

King Saul was not only disobedient to God, but he also had a mean streak. That was evident in the way Saul tormented David. It's as though Saul, even though he was tormented himself, wanted to **be** a tormentor. He wanted to and he did torment David.

Just know, any of us who are moving in unforgiveness, bitterness, resentment, vengeance, that the evil plans that we prepare for another person will roll back on us. It's not worth it. Don't be the power struck type, let Jesus take care of your vengeance needs. Do you want to *be* a tormentor and have already started devising plans for revenge? Then trust this, **YOU WILL BE TORMENTED**.

Are you determined to pay people back for wrongs you *think* they've done to you? Whoever digs a pit, will fall into that pit himself. Anybody who rolls a stone, get ready for the rollback. You better be careful. It always happens. Nobody escapes this.

The Stone Rolled Back

Some years ago, I was accused, by a power struck person, of something that I **did not do**. I really thought this person was my friend. They made this accusation so I would get into trouble--, and I did.

I thought this person was my friend, and he often mentioned God. I cannot judge if he was a friend of God's, but he was not really my friend, I found out later on. I don't know if you want to call him an unfriendly friend, I'd rather just call him an enemy right now.

This guy's accusation turned me over to tormentors, in the natural and that was his goal—or something worse, I've also come to learn.

No, I didn't go to a physical prison, but I was tormented because his actions sent me into a place of mental anguish where I suffered mental noise, asking myself repeatedly, *What did I do? How did I get accused of this? Why did this person do this to me?*

This is what I thought about around the clock--, and that is **torment**. I wallowed and wandered some months in that torment. I had to pray, pray my way out of it. Thankfully, the Lord brought me out of it.

Years went by before I even told this story. Then, since first telling this story, more time has gone by. Now, I have an update on being turned over to the ***tormentors*** in the natural world, by this former friend. That person accused me for no good reason of something totally unreasonable, and I was subjected to tormenting scrutiny. I knew I would be cleared of the accusations, but I had to go through the process. The process was tedious. The process was expensive; it cost me thousands of dollars and hours and hours of missed time from work. It cost me stress and worry. It was humiliating and inconvenient.

I add here, I had tried to and had been a *help* to this person while they seemed to be going through a hard time in their own life. When it was time for me to leave the location where he was, that person did not want me to leave, and the accusations were his retaliation for me leaving. Oh, and he owed me money.

I felt that he carried a *spirit of rejection,* but we were not interpersonal friends, it was nothing like that. Later I found that he had done similar retaliatory things to other people who "left" him, but not on the level he was doing it to me.

Approximately a year after his scathing accusations I was cleared of them. Approximately five years after that,

God declared judgment on that person. I had not prayed a judgmental prayer against the person, I never asked the Lord for vengeance or to do anything to this person. During those days I was more likely to ask the Lord to make it **stop** more so than **stop** the person, or even stop the *spirit* behind the person's behavior.

I did, however, pray, Psalm 105: *Touch not mine anointed do my prophet no harm* while standing on any paper document that had been sent to me, that had anything to do with this issue.

I never allowed any paperwork that had anything to do with the lies against me to be any higher than UNDER MY FEET. I proclaimed to the Lord that this matter would remain under my feet and have no higher position or standing in my life.

That person is dead. Buried.

That's how I know the Lord declared judgement. I was shocked when I found out he was dead. When I first shared this story, I did not know he was deceased. I had lost touch with him as soon as he accused me. Years had passed. And I only found out some years after about his death that his friends and family called *untimely*.

Did he do that to me and others because he was evil? Did it try to stick because *I* had it coming—, from bloodline issues? Neither you nor I should play the guilt-filled victim. We will just go into warfare and fire prayers and handle these matters in the Spirit.

Unforgiveness Has Torment

If torment is in your life, are you tormenting yourself? Are you bringing torment on yourself? This can happen when the trauma or the mind games that others are playing get into your head. This can happen if a trauma thrusts you into survival mode, for example.

Are you a victim of torment by enemies, careless people, unfriendly friends, or evil entities? Please don't be involved in helping mental weapons formed against you to prosper by dwelling on negativities and *what ifs* all day.

If you harbor unforgiveness, that's an engraved invitation for Torment to come into your life. A divorced person stuck in unforgiveness, bitterness and resentment toward their Ex will *invite* Torment. In that case, Torment has license and a wide-open door to vex you 24/7. Torment uses anyone, everyone--, most often, whomever is the closest, maybe even your kids.

Unforgiveness has torment. People who don't forgive can have the fear that if they forgive somebody, they will become a doormat or a laughingstock and they will be disrespected all the more. Worrying about what people think of you, constantly being on guard is also Torment. Unforgiveness has torment because people who don't forgive believe the attack will happen over and again. This ***fear*** puts them in survival mode, which perpetuates torment.

Sin has torment. Adam and Eve got kicked out of the Garden at Eden into toil, sweat, and adversity, straight into the

curse of the law of sin and death. Somewhere between sin and death there will be Torment.

Prison

Agree with an adversary quickly, whilst thou art in the way with him, lest at anytime the adversary deliver thee to the judge, and the judge deliver thee to the officer, and you'll be cast into prison, (Matthew 5:25).

The soul can be in prison. In the case where I was falsely accused, I didn't actually go to a physical prison. The torment was in my mind. I am more than certain that I didn't do anything to this person. I thought they were my friend. I was so angry I wanted to call him up and say a few things to him, but --

NO!

Acting on all or any of the impulses and feelings that are being sent to you by the chief tormentor, himself --the devil, would be the worst thing you could do in this situation. The devil is hoping you'll act on them, hoping you'll sin, hoping he will drag you all the way into the flesh, and that you'll jump into even a bigger sin. The little *tormenting spirits* create a constant drip, drip, drip. The goal is to nag you and push you to commit a big sin that lets a demonic *prince* into your life. Do not be deceived, in Jesus Name.

All the while you're feeling terrible because of these torments. You can't sleep, you don't want to sleep, *or* you want to sleep *all the time.* Life is going by, but you are not accomplishing anything. Your mind, which is part of your soul is being tortured and tormented; it is in a prison.

David, asked God, *How long are you going to leave my soul in prison?*

Maybe the answer is until you learn your lesson, or until you learn your lesson **and repent**. Or maybe the answer is until you learn your lesson, repent and get all of that evil out of your heart.

The part that you sin with is the part that the devil definitely has access to and often uses against you. It could be that he can use the part that your ancestors sinned with in the case of bloodline iniquity opening the door to him. We may only know that by God's Spirit.

Psalm 142 tells of a person's soul being in prison. A soul gets into a prison by his own sin, or because of ancient bloodline sin.

Emotional adultery is still sin. Emotional sin, when you are planning evil against somebody, either for payback or just because you don't like them. That's an emotional sin, and this invites torment into your life. Torment will arrive to torment you emotionally.

There are sins of the will--, things that you actually do--, transgressions.

Thinking on evil all the time is sin of the intellect. These are sins because the Word says you are to love the Lord with our whole soul. We don't parse out parts of our soul using it for fun over here with one part of it. We don't choose to do evil with another part of it, such as think on things we wish we could do to people, and then plan to go to church with another part.

Soul Ties

I talk about soul ties often—because there are levels of revelation in this. Soul ties, soulish prayers, soulish covenants all bring on torment. There is torment in a soul tie, even if you are tied for what you think is a good reason, such as ~~, you believe you love them so much.

The person that you are soul tied to is constantly on your mind. *What are they doing? What's he doing? What's she doing? Who's he with? Why aren't they calling me or answering my text?* This is all mental anguish. It's torment.

The gas lighter, the love bomber, the breadcrumber, the narcissist in interpersonal relationships –they are all Tormentors.

Listen, if a person can't talk to you like a normal human being, then you don't have a relationship. If you don't have a relationship, keep it moving. Keep it moving. God's got something better for you. God never does away with the first except to establish the second, which will always be better. Always. Amen.

So why are you standing still? That person that you're trying to be soul tied to has obviously moved on. The devil is in every soul tie. The devil is in every evil covenant. Once the devil is *in*, he can send in other *spirits*. He can send in Torment; and so he does.

I'm not just talking about interpersonal relationships, but there can be torment in family and friend connections, as well.

Your child is going off to college. Live your life. Do some new things in your life. Don't go into a pity party because you now feel as though you're alone, or you and your spouse are all alone. Your child has gone off to college. You are *not* supposed to be soul tied to your children. When they leave that will lead to bitterness.

Here's the part we really need to get. Torment has an open door, through unforgiveness, bitterness, soul ties, resentment, jealousy, envy, any evil work. These are the symptoms; these are some of the things that they cause: confusion, relationship instability, disappointment, unnecessary fights and arguments. Torment can lead to untimely death. Tormenting *spirits* are sent to accomplish just that kind of evil. All the while, you're feeling agitated, aggravated, disrespected, and/or ignored.

Even simple things will annoy you. Let's say you're in a traffic jam, so you move into the lane that's moving faster. As soon as you do, that lane slows down or comes to a complete stop. The lane you *were* in is now going faster.

That's torment.

Grocery store checkout line-- same thing. Inconveniently a price check is needed, or the cash register breaks or now the person's got to change the register, count the drawer, and change to a new clerk. You're standing there tapping your foot because you have to go.

Torment.

Or you get to the register and all of a sudden, they just close the lane on you. It just closes right in front of your face. More Torment.

At your job, you get written up because you're late for work. You don't get the raise that you know you're supposed to get. You've been disappointed at the edge of breakthrough. These are torments.

Your kids are at home acting up because that *spirit* is not just in you or on you, **it's in your house** agitating your spouse and your kids. Everybody's on edge even though they may not know why.

Anything that can go wrong just seems to go wrong. These are tormenting *spirits*, and if it weren't for bad luck, somebody tried to say that to me the other day about their life~~~, I stopped them. I wouldn't let them say the rest of it, none of us need to say that sort of thing. It draws negativity to us. All this is torment. *A man can have what he says.*

What torments you? Well, the devil knows, because he's been monitoring me, you, all of us, since we were born. Unless we do something about it.

- Lord in the Name of Jesus, every monitoring mirror or other device, electronic, energetic, or otherwise used to monitor me right now, catch fire and be blinded forever, in the Name of Jesus.
- Every monitoring agent assigned to monitor my life, go blind and forget

all you saw. Die now, in the Name of Jesus.

There are demons and evil *spirits* all around us that are looking for an opportunity to afflict and torment people. It is their assignment. It is their only assignment.

Constant guilt trips are another sign that a person is being oppressed by tormenting *spirits*. You feel guilty or restless, regretful, often. You may experience a feeling of weakness, or insecurity. Or, you could be feeling uncertain, or confused.

You could be having weird accidents or incidents. Bad dreams plague you. You may lose money or have business lags, for no obvious reason.

Unfortunately, there's more; it can get worse. You can't sleep, or you can't *stay* asleep. You're exhausted.

Things in your body start hurting.

You start stress eating. Yeah, that's not just craving comfort food--, that is stress eating. Then you're eating the wrong stuff, the inflammation-causing foods. If this doesn't stop, next comes the weight gain, feeling sluggish. So you try to comfort yourself with more of the food, drugs, sex—whatever you do to self-medicate. This perpetuates the cycle.

We all need Jesus to get us out of this mess if we find ourselves in this mess.

The Thing I Greatly Feared

For the thing which I greatly feared is come upon me, and that which I was afraid of is come unto me. Job 3:25

Torment is part of a downward spiral. You may start to lose friends. You don't want to do much of what you used to do anymore. You may jump into survival mode.

When attacks and afflictions come upon you, like Job you may also think or say, *The thing that I greatly feared has come upon me.*

Because fear has torment, the thing that you greatly fear comes upon a person because the devil knows what you greatly fear and your thinking on it constantly draws it to you. The devil has been studying you all your life. An attack is a custom-made **weapon** programmed against a person.

Greatly fearing and also regular fear both have Torment.

Fear tries to come into anybody's life and is often successful. Sometimes it comes by just a suggestion, or a sudden terror, incident, or trauma. If we don't apply the Blood of Jesus and the Word of God, we may start to think that this is the new norm, that this is it's how it's always going to be. If a person accepts fear, they will drive themselves further into fear and then fear opens the door for Torment to come in.

Fear has torment. If fear comes in, torment is right with it.

The Word of God says that we are to *think on these things.*

> And finally, brothers, whatever is true, whatever is honorable, whatever is right, whatever is pure, whatever is lovely. Whatever is admirable, if anything, is excellent and praiseworthy, think on these things. And whatever you've learned or received or heard from me or seen in me, put it into practice, and the God of peace will be with you.

Think on the things that God said for you to think on, because if you put your powerful mind on all of these possible *what ifs* and terrible disaster scenarios, you will draw that stuff to yourself. But mostly you put yourself in fear and that brings torment into your life.

The well-ordered, mature soul is disciplined, and it does not think on negative and evil things. Instead, the mind of that soul thinks on things that are lovely and pure, things that have good report, are honorable, and have virtue. We have a responsibility to guard our eyes, ears, and mind with all diligence, for out of our heart come the issues of life.

We have to resist delving into *wishcraft* where we are wishing, wishing, wishing. One such thing might be wishing that somebody that we've soul tied ourselves to would come back. It is blind witchcraft when we don't even realize that this is still witchcraft. Don't do this; God hates witchcraft of this kind, as well as full blown, blatant witchcraft.

Following other kinds of religions is also idolatry. This is not of God. Trying to manifest ungodly things really means you're **conjuring** up things--, things you may realize too late that you don't even want.

The things that thrill you today may kill you tomorrow. Horror movies--, some people say they like being scared, but why open the door for fear, since fear has torment? And how easy is it for you to forget a sudden terror? Sometimes it's very difficult. I meet people every day who are reliving their scary dental appointment from when they were 5 or 10. That was a sudden terror. They are now 40 years old and it's as vivid as yesterday to them.

Fear presents itself in all kinds of ways. Let's say you're at church and you're scared that people know that you really just don't like *her*. Who is she--, this "*her*"? I don't know, maybe she's another parishioner on the pew with you. To cover up not liking her, you start *acting* like you like this person, or else people will think you're not a good Christian if you don't like *her*. So you pretend to like somebody you don't really like. That's also torment. You fear, you're afraid that somebody will find out.

Acting as though you like somebody won't make it so. It makes you a hypocrite. It is a shame when you can't be yourself in life, in your marriage, at your job, and also at church.

If this persists, then you may start avoiding church. You may be asking, *Do we have to go there again?* Why do we have to go to lunch with *them* after church today? People of God, listen to your spouses. Do not put your spouse in a situation that torments them. That's cruel.

Parents, listen to your kids, your kids may be trying to avoid a bully. Bullies promote fear, and fear has torment. The devil is a bully.

There's mega emotional trauma involved in either of these cases. The devil uses trauma to open doors to get into your life.

Unforgiveness brings captivity; captivity brings torment. The tormentor is the jailer. A locked-up soul is in prison and that prison is in hell. Read: **Devil Weapons: Anger, Unforgiveness & Bitterness**, by this author. https://a.co/d/24biah2

Fragmented Soul

> Lord, have mercy upon me. O Lord, I'm weak. Oh Lord, heal me, for my bones are vexed, that is tormented. My soul is also sore, vexed, also tormented. But thou, O Lord, how long? Return O Lord, deliver my soul. Oh, save me for thy mercy sake,
>
> (Psalm 6:2-4).

How long? David wants to know, *Lord, are you going to leave my soul in hell?*

If *parts* of your soul are locked up in hell, you have a fragmented soul, you have a sold-out soul, and/or you have a soul tied soul. All soul tied souls are fragmented.

Soul tie covenants are all executed in Hell.

The devil is the executor over evil contracts.

Did you mean to get the devil into your contract, into your business, into your life? Did you mean to get into a contract with the devil? I never have. I've never meant to do it.

Lord, forgive us, in Jesus Name. We must pray.

If your soul is in hell, you're a prisoner. You are tied, shackled, and imprisoned. Unless you have *accepted* being there; do you like it there? If not, then why do you willfully tie yourself by perpetuating a soul tie? Perhaps you don't even **know** that you are imprisoned, and you think this is the way it's supposed to be; it's not.

A soul tie could be because of somebody you can't get over. It could be anyone or anything that you're obsessed about. You might as well just get the zip ties yourself and pull them tight through your teeth. Pining away and excessive grief both create soul ties.

I'm not judging anybody. I've done a lot of this stuff myself and I know what it's gotten me. I'm sharing so you can avoid some pain. It's gotten me nothing other than a waste of time, a waste of life and unnecessary torments that could have been avoided.

Hear the Word of the Lord today. Amen.

Closure

A person could be soul tied to anything or anyone. I lived in a house that we put on the market for sale, but I didn't think I was finished living in it yet, but we sold it and moved. Once I had moved, the Lord told me to withdraw my spirit from that house.

This is why I say goodbye to places when I move away from them. I say goodbye to people. It doesn't have to be face to face. But I do say it in prayer or in the Spirit.

Sometimes that provides the closure that people think and say they want. A person doesn't have to be right in front of you for you to get closure with them. If you went into your own house on a rainy day or snowy day, you would close the door behind yourself, wouldn't you? Would you wait for somebody else to come and do it? No, you'd close it yourself.

You want closure? Close the door yourself. I admonish you to close all open doors to your life that should not be open. That's another thing that prayer can do for you. The Holy Spirit is our seal – the Holy Spirit will help you close doors and Seal them that no person or demon can open again.

Withdraw yourself, withdraw your spirit from the business location that you *used to have* or work at. Withdraw your spirit from old and bad relationships, be they family, friendships, or interpersonal.

Withdraw your foot, lest your neighbor hate you. Shake the dust. Stop yearning over the good old days. Al Bundy needs to withdraw his 50-year-old spirit from his old high school, especially from the football games of yesteryear.

It took me some time to realize that I was soul tied over an old college relationship. I had prayed and prayed about it. I renounced it. I did everything I was supposed to do—everything that I knew to do at the time.

Then one day it became crystal clear to me that I really wasn't pining away for the *person*, or the relationship itself. I really just liked **myself** much better then. Life was easier. I was younger. I could lose weight *by Friday* if I wanted to. I had lots of social events on my calendar. I could stay up late, and not be tired the next day. I could get out of bed, and nothing would hurt. What a revelation that was to me. I had to pray to break the soul tie to that *time period* of my life!

I hope that blesses somebody today.

So don't soul tie yourself to the past. Don't soul tie yourself to a person, place, or time. Thank God for the days of your youth and move on to bigger and better things, in the Name of Jesus.

When you obsess over people, they can feel it on some level. Truthfully, if they want to be around you, they would be, if they could be. If not, you're really doing one of two things—or perhaps both things--, you're pushing them further and further away from you. Or, if they can't be with you--, you're drawing something evil to yourself because it's soulish, and God's not in that.

So if you keep obsessing over them, it is a sin of the soul, and the devil will send you something *like* what you think you want. It might look like it, it might walk like it, it might talk like it-- at first, let's say, in your dream life. If you agree to one of these types of dreams, or if you do nothing, get ready because you could be inviting torment into your life and when it gets there, it will want to *marry* you. Whether you agree to it or not, whether you know it or not. This is called a *spirit spouse.*

More on this in my book, **Fantasy Spirit Spouse**, https://a.co/d/beDEPFy

Because God knows how powerful He made your mind, He said, *Think on these things*, because as a man thinketh, so is he, and he also can draw things to himself. Some call it manifesting, but if God's not in it, if the devil gets in it, it's ***conjuring***.

When you make these soul covenants and soulish prayers and you have your soulish desires, you could be conjuring. This is witchcraft--, **wishcraft**, if you think it's innocent. Whatever you open the door to, that's what will come in. If you establish soulish contracts, soulish covenants, especially by soulish prayers and desires, you've invited the devil in and whatever demons he can get into your life to torment you.

Unless you get rid of it, Torment is on the menu. If you forget to get rid of it because maybe it slipped in and hid, it's in your *generations* now, waiting for your kids. Who knows when your kids or your grandkids are *going through* if they will ever figure out where this torment that is afflicting their lives came from. They could be frustrated for years or decades asking themselves, *Why am I going through this? Why does this horrible stuff keep happening?*

They may never figure it out, but instead, just suffer. And, they will have you to thank.

You might have inherited spiritual junk yourself that you may be trying to figure out. You may be asking, *why is this happening*, because you're sure you haven't done anything to deserve *this*.

It could be coming from the foundation you may have inherited by the family that you were born into. What ancestral covenants and curses and torments were there already? Torment is not a one and done. It's perpetual and it's most inconvenient. It's stressful, it's straining, it's distressing and draining; it's defeat at the edge of success. It's a disappointment over and over. It brings sleepless nights because of your own thoughts or thoughts that are being inserted into the dream or into your mind. Torment can come in the form of dreams that haunt or terrorize your life.

Torment --, that odd and sudden sound in your house. Things go bump in the night, and you know you heard that. It's all that stuff that Psalm 91 can help you settle. Go ahead and pray; it will protect you from all that, in Jesus' Name. When you hear those odd sounds, rise up and speak to Torment. In the whole armor of God and covered by the Blood of Jesus, tell Torment to cease and desist. Tell it that it has no place in your home and tell it to leave your house, and never return, by the power in the Name of Jesus.

Torment is pain and suffering; it is annoyance. It's anxiety. It's like a toothache, an earache or a constant drip from the bathroom sink and you're trying to sleep. It's torture. It's a backache. These things are greatly painful. Torment is getting exactly what you *don't* want.

I'm sorry, Doctor Seuss, it's like the Cat in the Hat, Thing One and Thing Two coming in to tear up your house. God is telling us not to invite trouble. Don't invite anybody evil to your house. Because it's much harder to get rid of them than it is to never invite them or to never conjure them up at all.

If you have the opportunity to forgive somebody, forgive them. Take the opportunity to release them. You live and let them live.

In the case of a lost loved one, you live and let them rest in peace. If you've ever lived in a house with a baby or someone who is napping, you let them rest. You don't selfishly kick up a ruckus and constantly make noise to disturb them. Let those who are resting, rest. Let them rest in peace.

Recommended: **Seasons of Grief** by this author. https://a.co/d/2YmJq7Z

Stay prayed up, stay in the Word, praise, worship. Honor God. Be filled and refilled with the Spirit of God so He is fully in you, and there's no place for the devil.

Give no place to the devil. Resist the devil, and he will flee from you. Do not entertain temptation. Do not invite a *guardian demon.* Leave evil Thing One, Two, Three and et cetera in hell or wherever they are. You don't want that in your life.

Torment can be physical, mental or both. It brings mental suffering, agony, misery, maybe both, as I said, and your soul could be in torment. Physical torments are illnesses and diseases.

Have you ever heard someone say, He/She is such a tormented soul. Yeah, that's a real thing.

How long? David wants to know, *how long is the Lord going to leave his soul in prison?*

There are people out here hunting souls, but that's another whole book. Don't just relinquish or hand your soul over.

Once captive, there will be torment, there will be torture. There are so many torture methods. The devil loves to inflict trauma, and he'll have it done to you by traumatic methods. He will not hesitate to use debilitating, scary methods of torture. **unless** you stop him. And you do that with your words, and with your prayers.

You haven't devised torture for vengeance against anybody, have you? Do not have a human object of your hatred; that is not of God. You don't know how much is the right amount of payback. Trust me, you don't. Humans most often go overboard with power. Get out of unforgiveness and plans of vengeance because the very thing you've devised for them is probably the exact thing that's going to happen to you.

Lord, have Mercy! It just dawned on me that the fellow who turned me over to the Tormentors had certain desires toward me and when the stone rolled back, that is what happened to him!

Saints of God, this is serious. Spiritual warfare is serious, it is important, and it is a battle, a war, and a matter of life and death. Be diligent in praying for yourself and for others.

God has told us what some of the torments are going to be--, pestilence, sickness, inflammation, and a closed Heaven. God's not even hearing your prayer anymore, drought. Your money gets funny for no apparent reason. Things break in the house. You will have to keep spending money on stuff that you hadn't planned to spend money on. These are torments the enemy brings. Oh, there's more--, hemorrhoids, itch, you might --as well say the *mange*, madness, blindness, astonishment of heart.

You get engaged and somebody steals your beloved--, yeah Torment brings heartbreak, heartache, rejection.

These are the assignments of tormenting *spirits*. They cause confusion and guilt. And they travel in bunches, there is not usually just one. Don't bullies travel together? They come in a cluster. They can cause you to get blamed for stuff you didn't even do. You can even get accused of *not* doing things. You may end up beating yourself up with self-talk such as, *I should have done this, I should have done that*. They accuse all the time—even false accusations.

These evil spirits are on assignment to destroy and to break a man down, like a meat tenderizer buffeting, beating a man down. They are doing all this groundwork to introduce a demonic **prince**, an entity with more authority and more power to do more harm to your life. They don't stop until and unless you **stop** them. We have to repent, turn to God and repent. It's the only way out.

They come to remind you of your past, guilt trip you, making you feel worse.

This may make you want revenge on that person you've chosen not to forgive.

As bad as all this is, a demonic prince is waiting in the wings if the tormenting *spirits* can beat you down enough. That demonic *prince* wants to come into your life, with the same assignment to steal, kill, and destroy, but this time on steroids.

Love Has No Torment

Wait a minute, didn't the opening verse say that perfect love casts out fear? Fear has torment but perfect love casts out fear?

> There is no fear in love; but perfect love casteth out fear: because fear hath torment. He that feareth is not made perfect in love.
>
> 1 John 4:18

Love is patient. Love is kind. Love does not envy. Love is not boastful. It's not proud. It doesn't dishonor others. It's not self-seeking, it's not easily angered. It keeps no record of wrongs. Look at that-- forgiveness. Love forgives. Love does not delight in evil. Love rejoices in the truth, it protects, it trusts, it is trustworthy, it hopes, and it perseveres. Love never fails.

No, I'm not doing a wedding ceremony here, but since our goal is marriage to the Lamb, we should be walking in this perfect love all the time. If we're walking in this perfect love and resisting the devil, the devil will flee from us with all of his demons, and we will not go through torment and be tormented.

Walking in agape love, our soul matures, it becomes a well-ordered soul, a well-disciplined soul that thinks on this and not that. We feed our soul this and not that, as the Lord says, not a steady diet of the World of Darkness and evil, but a steady diet of the Word and praise and worship.

Torment is really a witchcraft spirit, and it's here to dominate, intimidate, manipulate, control, steal, kill, destroy.

When the torment is too much, when you've had enough, let's pray.

Warfare Prayers

Holy Spirit, fall on us now. Build a wall of Fire, a hedge of Fire, a mountain of Fire around us for protection now, in the Name of Jesus.

Lord, I ask for the protection of the Blood of Jesus Christ over myself and these prayers, in Jesus' Name.

In the Name of Jesus Christ and by the power of His Blood, I bind the power of every evil *spirit*, especially tormenting *spirits*, and command that they will not block this prayer--, these prayers, in the Name of Jesus.

Lord, I forgive everyone who has offended, hurt, harmed, traumatized me in any way my entire life, in the Name of Jesus.

I do not forgive any evil entities, *spirits*, principalities, spiritual wickedness in high places, rulers in darkness, evil *spirits* or any unrepentant human agents who have made themselves my adversaries and seek after my life.

I command you, devil not to interfere with this prayer. You will not stir up grief, fear of any kind, or emotional trauma against me. I command quiet, in the Name of Jesus.

Jesus, take the sting, the bite the hurt, the pain, the loss out of every betrayal, assault, or attack against me, so it no longer harms me, and I don't draw evil to myself, especially any tormenting *spirits*, by reliving it, by continuing to think on it by unforgiveness, resentment, bitterness or planning revenge, in Jesus' Name.

Lord, release me from the hell of soul captivity and imprisonment, by the Blood of Jesus, in the Name of Jesus.

Every power tormenting me since I was born, die in the Name of Jesus.

Every power tormenting my health, finances, relationships, including destiny helpers, Lord Jesus contend with them, torment them back, in the Name of Jesus.

The Blood of Jesus! The Blood of Jesus! The Blood of Jesus! I plead the Blood of Jesus.

Every tormenter of my life, die in the Name of Jesus.

As the Lord has power on Earth to forgive sin, let me forgive all those who have sinned against me, knowing that they've really sinned against You and that vengeance is Yours, not mine. You'll repay. I don't need to devise any plans, schemes, or evil against anyone, in the Name of Jesus.

In the Name of Jesus, I resist the *spirit of the avenger*. I shall not take vengeance into my own hands, but I will allow the Holy Spirit and God's mighty angels to fight and win my battles, in Jesus Name.

Lord, thank You for divine vengeance and vindication, in the Name of Jesus.

Lord, help me, show me how to forgive all those who I even *think* have sinned against me, in the Name of Jesus.

Lord, I cancel all evil plans, schemes, and devices that I've thought of or set in motion against anyone. Please forgive me, in the Name of Jesus.

I repent of the same and I repent of *wish*craft, blind witchcraft any and all witchcraft, under the guise of feeling hurt or feeling like I'm a victim. Lord, forgive me. None of that justifies any evil or wicked schemes. Lord, forgive me and have mercy on me, deal with me mercifully, in Jesus' Name.

I bind up the powers of Earth, air, water, fire in the netherworld, and the satanic forces of nature. I break all curses, hexes, vexes, jinxes, spells, and any sorcery against me, and I declare them null and void, in Jesus' Name.

I break every evil covenant, contract, soul tie, and devil deal, be it recent or ancestral, in the Name of Jesus.

I demolish every evil altar working against me, and my life with the Thunder Fire of God.

I demolish every evil altar that is emanating evil against me, and I bind the strongman and I send them to the true Lord Jesus for ministry. Lord, rule over them with an iron rod if they do not accept repentance, in the Name of Jesus.

I break every evil curse that keeps any evil covenant in place, working against me. I bind every devil assigned to enforce every curse against me, in the Name of Jesus.

I cancel every assignment of every evil *spirit*, and I command all their assignments that are against me, to expire, in the Name of Jesus.

Father, bless all humans who do not know any better, by sending your Holy Spirit to lead them to conviction, repentance and conversion, in the Name of Jesus. Those who do know better and choose to continue doing wrong, I commend them into Your Hands, Mighty God.

Lord, I do not bless any unrepentant evil enemies--, human or otherwise who are bent on my death or destruction. Lord, contend with them that contend with me, deal with them as they have dealt with me, in the Name of Jesus.

To all unrepentant determined evil agents out to kill me or destroy my life, I forgive you, but I send it all your evil back to you. Back to sender, in Jesus' Name.

I will not die. I shall live and declare the goodness of the Lord in the land of the living, in the Name of Jesus. Receive the vengeance of the Lord who says, *"Touch not mine anointed, do my prophet no harm."*

I bind all interaction and communication in the world of evil *spirits* as it affects my life, family, career, business, education, marriage, ministry, all things that I have stewardship over, in the Name of Jesus.

I command all organized forces of darkness working against my life to receive lightning and Thunder, in the Name of Jesus.

Every arrow coming from automatic networks against me, miss your target, and back to sender, in the Name of Jesus.

I command all demonic organizers, networks, agents working in my life spiritually to scatter by Holy Ghost Fire, in the Name of Jesus.

Lord, thank You for Your protection and sending Your warrior angels to give me victory in this battle. Do not leave my soul in hell, Father. I scatter all spiritual, physical, and energetic padlocks, fetters, chains, crystal balls, basins, pins, knives, weapons, images, caricatures, idols and effigies used against me in the satanic world, in the Name of Jesus.

I command fire upon every satanic beast and satanic paraphernalia, witch's covens, satanic groves, altars, trees, rocks, stones, dirt, air, water, celestial bodies, marine dwellings, and shrines where my name has been called, is being called, or shall ever be called for evil, in any era, age, timeline, realm, dimension, past, present and future, to infinity, in the Name of Jesus.

Wherever my name has been called or is being called, or shall ever be called for evil, in any era, age, timeline, realm, dimension, past, present and future, to infinity, Blood of Jesus, answer for me, in the Name of Jesus.

I scatter every arrest warrant issued against my life in the spirit realm, in Jesus' Name.

Any evil entity assigned to announce my obituary in the spirit, find me not. Announce your own obituary, I shall live and not die, and declare the goodness of the Lord, in the Land of the Living, in Jesus' Name.

I nullify every spiritual surveillance over my life, family, job and business. Lord, blind every eye of every *monitoring spirit*, and deafen their ears to my every word, in the Name of Jesus.

I release myself from every lawful and unlawful captivity of satanic principalities and powers, by the Blood of Jesus.

I bind, destroy, denounce, renounce and nullify every covenant, soul tie I have made, knowingly or unknowingly with Satan's principalities, powers, rulers of darkness, spiritual wickedness in high places, *familiar spirits, monitoring spirits,* witches of any kind, wizards, or any evil human agent, in the Name of Jesus.

I scatter every fowler's snare set against my life, in the Name of Jesus.

I scatter horses sent against me, in the Name of Jesus.

I declare that Jesus has redeemed me from every captivity and Curse of the Law when He hung on the Cross, He died for me, thank You Lord, and was resurrected.

Because I'm more than a conqueror, no weapon formed against me shall prosper or get to its target, I thwart every evil arrow and dart with the Shield of Faith, in the Name of Jesus.

Every enemy and satanic scheme to destabilize my progress is found and cancelled and burned past recognition with Holy Ghost Fire, in Jesus' Name.

I'm free. Because the Truth, the Word, Jesus Christ, the Blood and the Anointing has set me free, indeed.

As a result of satanic captivity, every evil covenant that is keeping every yoke and burden in place against me is destroyed and lifted from me now, in Jesus' Name.

In the Name of the Lord Jesus Christ, I claim full victory that Christ won over Satan and his demons at the Cross.

In the Name of Jesus Christ I take back all ground ever given to Satan and break every evil hold over my mind, my body, and my life.

Father, release Your fire --I need solution to this problem, in the Name of Jesus.

My life receive fire, become fire in the Name of Jesus. (X5)

Every ancestral power of my father's house, mother's house and my environment that says I will not receive my freedom, die in the Name of Jesus.

I resist the devil and his demons and command them to flee. Tormenting demons, I bind you with chains of fire. I command you to be silent; I am a child of Almighty God purchased by the Blood of Jesus Christ.

I've been delivered from the Kingdom of Darkness and translated into the Kingdom of His beloved Son, Jesus Christ.

I've been crucified with Christ. Nevertheless. I live yet not I, but Christ who lives in me and the life I live by faith in the Son of God, who loved me and gave His life for me. He made us alive together with Him and raised me up into heavenly places. The Lord Jesus Christ, far above all principalities and powers--, I claim for myself, the mind of Christ and the peace of Christ that surpasses all understanding.

I set the Blood of Christ Jesus against every demon, and I prevent them from intruding into my mind, my life, and my body, in Jesus' Name.

Holy Spirit, strengthen me spiritually so I can withstand the forces of darkness today.

As the righteousness of God, I claim my household totally consecrated for the Kingdom of God, therefore the scepter of evil cannot and will not invade the *land* that the Lord has given me, in the Name of Jesus.

Every evil *spirit* that does not have legal ground to be here go immediately to the pit, in the Name of the Lord Jesus Christ.

I revoke every legal right that I've given to any evil *spirit*, demon, principality, power or any other evil entity be it *spirit*, human, any part human, hybrid, or synthetic. I revoke any and every legal right that I've given them to be here and operate here, in the Name of Jesus.

I revoke it. NOW!

Blood of Jesus. Cry me out of every ground that I've given to the devil in my ignorance, rebellion, or disobedience, in the Name of Jesus.

Heavenly Father, have your warring angels take away all the evil demons, but Lord leave mighty angels remain here for protection of this place in time of warfare.

Thank You, Lord. I pray that You place a hedge of protection around this home. Lord, stand angels at every dimensional access point to my dwelling place, and my life, in the Name of Jesus.

I dedicate my life to You. I rededicate my life to You, Lord, for the Kingdom of the Almighty God and His Son, the Lord Jesus Christ.

I ask these things in the blessed Name of my Savior, the Lord Jesus Christ, and I believe that I receive what I ask. Amen.

Father, thank You for rising to torment and conquer all those who torment me, in the Name of Jesus.

All powers from the pit of hell tormenting me, die, in the Name of Jesus.

Thank You, Lord. For perfecting me in love, showing me patience, kindness, and all the Fruit of the Spirit, in the Name of Jesus.

Lord, take away envy, boastfulness, and pride from me and bind them from operating in my life, in the Name of Jesus.

Father, let me not dishonor others or seek vain glory or my own way. I bind the *spirits* of anger and wrath, in the Name of Jesus.

I keep no record of wrongs done, in the Name of Jesus.

I do not delight in evil, but in Your Word and in Truth, in Jesus Name.

Lord, make me complete in You, in the Name of Jesus.

I declare that every tormenting *spirit* of infirmity that has deposited sickness inside of me, by the power of God, consume it with Your hottest flames, and flush it out of my system, with Living Water, in the Name of Jesus.

The assignments of every evil *spirit* that is sent to deposit sickness, the Lord Jesus rebuke you, take you away to the pit for early torment. I declare: **FAILED ASSIGNMENT**, in the Name of Jesus.

I vomit out all evil *spirit* food from the night caterers, and night raiders, in the Name of Jesus. Lord Jesus, heal me of every evil effect of evil consumption, eaten in ALL OF MY LIFE, in the Name of Jesus.

Lord, make me complete in You, in the Name of Jesus. Thank You, Lord, that I'm no longer a child and I do not think childishly. I am not mentally, emotionally or spiritually childish, in the Name of Jesus.

Lord, Thank You for a mature, well-ordered soul, so that I can serve You with my **whole** soul, in the Name of Jesus.

Thank You, Lord.

Lord, by the reason of Your Blood, thank You for destroying every work of the devil in my life, in the Name of Jesus.

Every demon responsible for delay and hold ups in my life, I bind you, in the Name of Jesus. You are cast out of my life, forever.

Every monitoring demon assigned to my life and family, I bind and cast you out of all your hidden places, forever, in the Name of Jesus.

Every difficult problem in my life receive solution now, in the Name of Jesus.

Lord, let my life and all that concerns may be too hot for the enemies of God, in the Name of Jesus.

Every invisible chain that has tied my legs to not move forward, or my hands to not receive good things-- break now, in the Name of Jesus. Break! Break! Break!

Every unclean *spirit* that has brought affliction into my life, GO in the Name of Jesus.

Every satanic word said concerning my life is reversed now, in the Name of Jesus.

I cancel every satanic instruction ever spoken to me, audibly, or subliminally and I purge my life of all of the evil effects of any evil instruction, by the Blood of Jesus.

Every negative pronunciation from the pit of hell and every divination working against my glory, I decree that you are reversed right now, in the Name of Jesus.

To every power that has marked me for poverty, untimely death, or backwardness: All those marks are now removed by the Blood of Jesus, in the Name of Jesus. Go your way and do not trouble me again.

I bind up every spirit of retaliation against me, my house, my family and these prayers, in the Name of Jesus.

Thank You, Lord, Thank You for hearing these prayers. I count it as done. Thank You, Lord Jesus.

Amen.

Dear Reader

Thank you for acquiring and reading this book. I pray that every torment will leave your life and your bloodline and you will enjoy the Peace of God that passes all understanding in your family for a thousand years.

Shalom,

Dr. Marlene Miles

Christian books by this author

These books were recommended in this volume. Find other Christian books by this author on amazon/Kindle and other platforms.

AK: Adventures of the Agape Kid

AMONG SOME THIEVES

As My Soul Prospers

Behave

Churchzilla (The Wanna-Be Bride of Christ)

The Coco-So-So Correct Show

Demons Hate Questions

Do Not Orphan Your Seed

Do Not Work for Money

Don't Refuse Me Lord

The FAT Demons

got Money?

Let Me Have a Dollar's Worth

Living for the NOW of God

Lord, Help My Debt

Lose My Location

Made Perfect In Love

The Man Safari *(Really, I'm Just Looking)*

Marriage Ed., *Rules of Engagement & Marriage*

The Motherboard: *Key to Soul Prosperity*

My Life As A Slave

Name Your Seed

Plantation Souls

The Poor Attitudes of Money

Power Money: Nine Times the Tithe

The Power of Wealth

Seasons of Grief

Seasons of War

SOULS in Captivity

Soul Prosperity: Your Health & Your Wealth

The *spirit* of Poverty

This Is *NOT* That

The Throne of Grace, *Courtroom Prayers*

Warfare Prayer Against Poverty

When the Devourer is Rebuked

The Wilderness Romance

Other Journals & Devotionals by this author:

The Cool of the Day – Journal for times with God

got HEALING? Verses for Life

got HOPE? Verses for Life

got LOVE? Verses for Life

He Hears Us, Prayer Journal *in 4 colors*

I Have A Star, Dream Journal

I Have A Star, Guided Prayer Journal, *2 styles:*

J'ai une Etoile, Journal des Reves

Let Her Dream, Dream Journal *multiple colors*

Men Shall Dream, Dream Journal, *(blue, black)*

My Favorite Prayers (in 4 styles)

My Sowing Journal (in three different colors)

Tengo una Estrella, Diario de Sueños

Wise Counsel Journal

Illustrated children's books by this author:

Big Dog (8-book series)

Do Not Say That to Me

Every Apple

Fluff the Clouds

Love You All Over the World

Imma Dance

The Jump Rope

Kiss the Sun

The Masked Man

Not During a Pandemic

Push the Wind

Tangled Taffy

What If?

Wiggle, Wiggle; Giggle, Giggle

Worry About Yourself

You Did Not Say Goodbye to Me

Notes

Notes

www.ingramcontent.com/pod-product-compliance
Lightning Source LLC
Chambersburg PA
CBHW071309040426
42444CB00009B/1950